CW00706884

SHADOWS OF BRIGHTNESS

STEPHEN JACKSON AND BRIAN WEXHAM

NHP
New Hobsons Press

© 1998 Brian Wexham and Steve Jackson
Film Produced by Prestige Colour
Published by
New Hobsons Press Pty Limited
ACN 055 719 947
(a division of APN Educational Media Pty Limited)
Level 4, 2 Elizabeth Plaza
North Sydney NSW
Australia 2060
Tel: (612) 9936 8630
Fax: (612) 9936 8631

Cataloguing in Publication data
    Wexham, Brian, 1948-.
    Shadows of Brightness

    ISBN 1 876196 20 3

    1.Kenya-Description and travel. 2.Kenya-Pictorial
    works. I.Jackson, Steve, 1947-. II.Title.

    916.762

Extracts from *I Dreamed of Africa* by Kuki Gallman (Viking 1991) reproduced by kind permission of Penguin Books Ltd

Printed by Toppan, Singapore

Designed by Kerry Klinner

For Jody, Meghan, Kelly, Kimberley and the children of Africa.

As I stand in the lamp's light —
and the daffodils are dying because of my crying, down by the lamps light ...
down by the lamps light

A proportion of the royalties from this book are being donated to Save the Children Fund and the Dr Jane Goodall Institute, a non-profit organisation devoted to conservation.

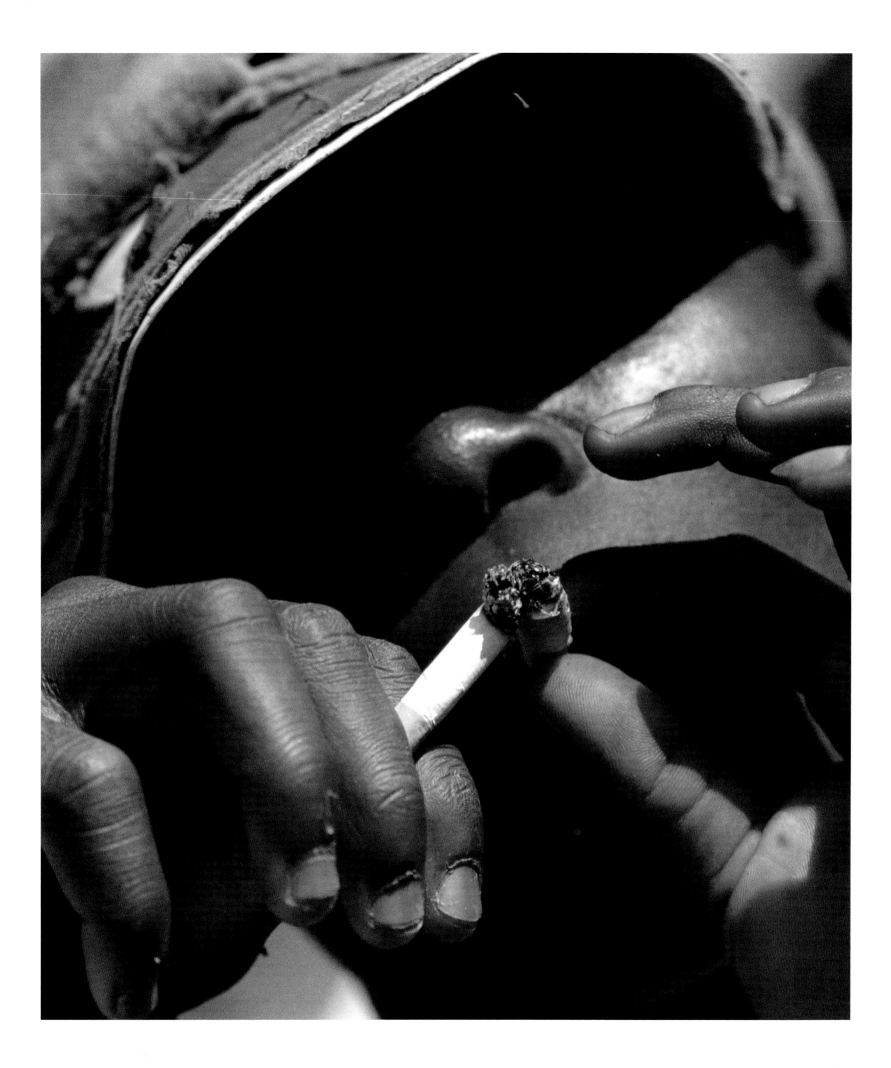

FOREWORD

Nairobi was my first port of call in Africa more than 30 years ago, and I still recall the magic of that first visit. It was 1963, the year of Uhuru, and Harold Macmillan's 'Wind of Change' was blowing warmly through the continent. I was on my way to Nyasaland, about to become the independent state of Malawi, where I had been invited to edit the local newspaper. For a young idealist, inspired on the flight over by reading Tom Mboya's autobiography, who believed Africans could make a better job of running their own countries than the colonialists ever had (a view not universally acknowledged in Britain at the time), bliss was it then to be alive and to be in Kenya was very heaven.

The trees in Nairobi shone with Jacaranda, Frangipani and Bougainvillea, none of which I had ever seen before. It was like a secret garden. Their scent was intoxicating, like the prevailing mood of hope and optimism in the country at large. I wandered happily round the streets of the capital; I went to see the beaches, which seemed like a tropical paradise; I travelled into the area of the Masai people; and I marvelled at the wonders of the game reserves. To someone from a damp and dispiriting British winter, the colours and the brightness were truly enchanting.

I have visited Kenya many times since, and although the country has experienced the problems of any developing country, the magic of that first introduction has never really worn off. It may be partly to do with the sense that in going to East Africa, scene of the historic archaeological digs by the Leakey family, one feels that one is revisiting the cradle of the human race.

Kenya's many and contrasting pleasures never cease to please and surprise. The beaches, the wildlife, the rugged highlands, the forests bursting with birdsong and insect noises, the desert, the rolling Savannah studded with lakes and volcanoes — all have their charms. Above all, though, it is the people of Kenya of whom one retains the most vivid memories.

Two visits stand out as memorable in my mind. One was my first trip to Mombasa, a city that seems to embody in itself the history not only of Kenya but the whole of Africa. Asian and Arab influences survive in the dozens of mosques and Sikh and Hindu temples in the winding streets of the old town, which slopes gently down to the once busy dhow harbour. The men and women go about in brightly coloured clothes you see nowhere else. On the coast itself, either south at Diani or north towards Malindi, there is a beguiling, steamy languor.

The other memory is of Masai Mara game reserve, close to the southwestern border with Tanzania, which has been described as 'the New York of the natural world'. It certainly seems as though the animals hold sway in the region — lions, elephants, buffalo, rhinos, cheetahs, leopards, hyenas, as far as the eye can see. The Mara river itself is full of hippos. Thousands of wildebeest cross the border every July and August from the Serengeti plain in Tanzania in a mass migration, eating their way north to the succulent green grass of the Mara.

This was the home of the Masai, Kenya's most romantic tribe, once great warriors, now the staple of the tourist trade. Tall and slender, decorated in bright jewellery and dressed in the brilliant red robes, they retain a dignity that seems to defy the modern world.

In this book, 'Shadows of Brightness', Brian Wexham and Steve Jackson have captured much of Kenya's charm and beauty. But they have hidden nothing. Every city has its dark corners, and they have paused to peer into some of these as well. The resulting portrait stands out from the tourist picture postcard view of Kenya: it is tough as well as tender; it is authentic; and, above all, it is African.

I have been privileged to meet many Kenyan leaders over the years. I was once invited to Nairobi by the Kenyan Government to lead a discussion with the local and international media about problems of perception faced by African countries. Many of them feel unjustly treated; they claim that the media concentrate too much on their faults and too little on their achievements; that they make too little effort to understand.

I tried to explain each side to the other, for I had experience of both, and I tried to use this experience to promote better mutual understanding. I don't know if I succeeded, but I have always felt a sense of personal honour and gratification that Kenya should have regarded me as a friend in this way. They were right to do so. It gives me great pleasure to commend the book that follows. I feel sure that it will make the country many more friends and also make it better understood. Few books can hope to do more.

Donald Trelford

ACKNOWLEDGMENTS

I am under the very greatest obligation to Steve Jackson for making his extensive library of photographs available to me, and for his invaluable help in preparing this book. I am also grateful to Kerry Klinner for her ready counsel and practical assistance and whose patience I have sorely tried over the past year.

To Donald Trelford, who has always been an inspiration to me, and to my numerous kindly hosts in Nairobi, whose ready co-operation enabled me to view for myself many of the locations featured in this book, my indebtedness is beyond adequate expression.

Finally, I wish to thank my children, who share my enthusiasm for Africa and who, during difficult times, were generous in every way, often providing the encouragement that kept me going.

Brian Wexham

INTRODUCTION

Writing an introduction to this selection of photographs is a task which should not, I realise, be treated with levity. To outsiders, Kenya has a surreal and romantic quality popularised by its abundance of wildlife and colonial past. This popularity, while providing a degree of economic security for Kenya's expanding population, has brought difficulties of some proportion. Yet Kenya also offers many indefinable qualities; images are thrust upon you so forcefully, leaving vivid memories. Who can forget in the heart of Nairobi the Kikuyu women, laden with excessive bundles of sticks, or the brightly coloured Matatus, enriched by their succinct slogans?

Inspiration prompts me to assemble these images. It is not a definitive collection, more a personal journey for the authors. The pictures are not about themes or messages of any kind except to say that people who live and suffer comprise the sum of anything worth writing about. People threatened by desperate or severe circumstances. These people are Africans. Despite their difficulties and the enormity of their task, their lives go boisterously on through adversity.

These photographs capture Kenya's subtle moods, its awesome views and the warmth and simplicity of the people. The pictures have a depth and honesty; some have humour. They show the dignity of the people, a quality intrinsic to them. They provide glimpses of a former age.

Africa is a land of extremes — romance, brutality, sheer self-indulgence. And at the end of an African day the night is illuminated by a million twinkling stars, a stillness followed by a dawn. A vivid explosion of colour. Magic sequences that provoke an involuntary gasp.

After putting out the paraffin lamp, I lay before sleep listening to a far-away hyena, giant croaking toads, strange rustles. A lion's sudden deep-throated roar, swallowing all other noises, was so startlingly close that the canvas seemed to vibrate at the sound. It was only my second night in Africa, yet something had begun to grow inside me which I could not stop, as if my childhood dreams had finally found the place where they could materialise. I had arrived where I was always meant to be. I did not know how it could be practically achieved, but I was certain beyond any shadow of doubt that it was here that I wanted to live.

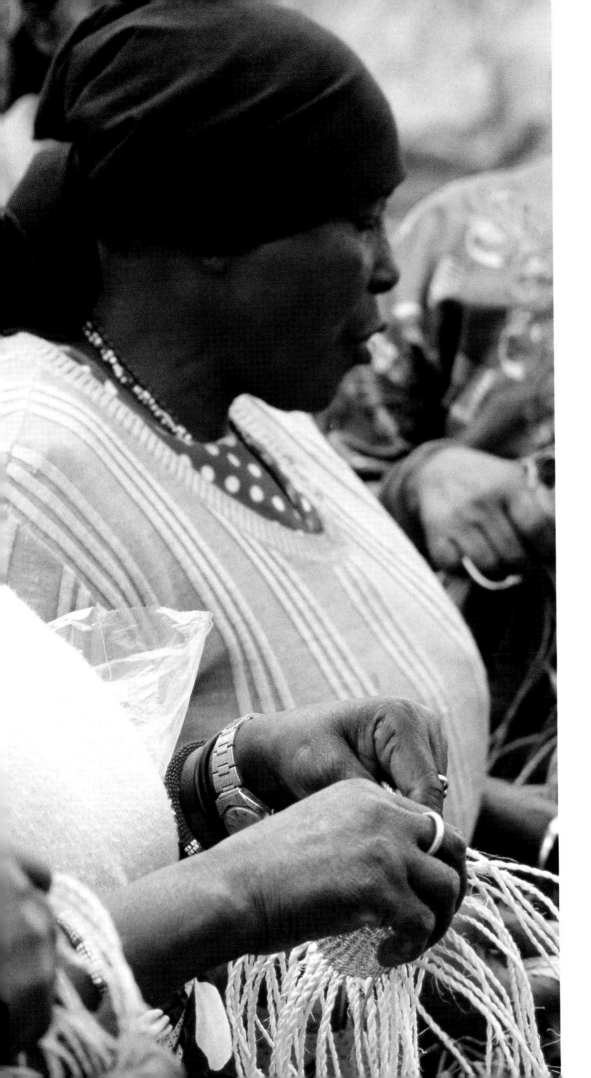

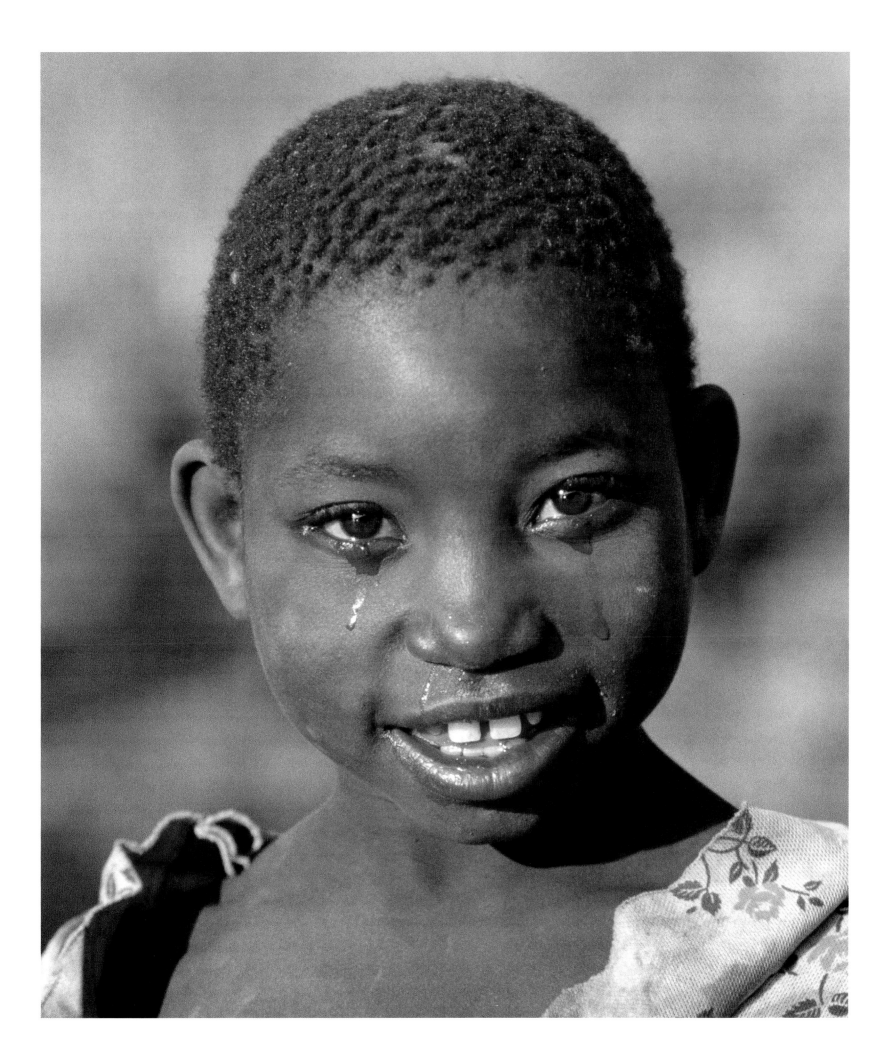

In Kenya, as elsewhere, the changes that have taken place this century have been immense, but the appeal remains. The graceful nomads with their herds of cattle and flocks of sheep and goats are largely untouched by the crude hand of contemporary civilization; the lovely hills and valleys, the spectacular landscape and the friendliness of the people are still there. Much, of course, has gone for ever. Great herds of wild animals have been ruthlessly destroyed; many of the wide, almost limitless, plains have been carved up into fields of crops and little homesteads; huge trees have been razed to the ground and forested river-banks laid bare; tarmac roads with roaring traffic have replaced the footpaths and game trails of the past. Yet, in the remoter areas, the sympathetic traveller can still experience something of the mystery and magic of Kenya.

KENYA THE FIRST EXPLORERS NIGEL PAVITT

Kobil
NAIROBI
KANGUNDO
PUMWANI GLASS HARDWARE MART LTD
PUMWANI GLASS HARDWARE MART LTD
KASILILI KA.IITUNE MINI BUS
P.S.V.
KOMWE WAA ATA ?
80
KWJ 270

In Africa age is equated with wisdom, since the original culture was the accumulated knowledge and skills which come only with experience and time. Old people were respected and honoured. Young people listened to them, and their advice was sought to solve quarrels and to pass judgement in all aspects of village life. Having gone through many seasons and listened to their fathers and grandfathers, they could foresee patterns in the rains and recognise early signs of drought. They knew the secrets of the animals and of the plants, the traditional herbal remedies, and the rituals to keep gods happy or to prevent their wrath. The elders were the library in which was stored all the knowledge the tribe needed to survive and to thrive. As in the herds of elephant, where it is the old matriarchs who lead the younger animals to the waterholes and the feeding grounds, the old people steered the village on to the right path.

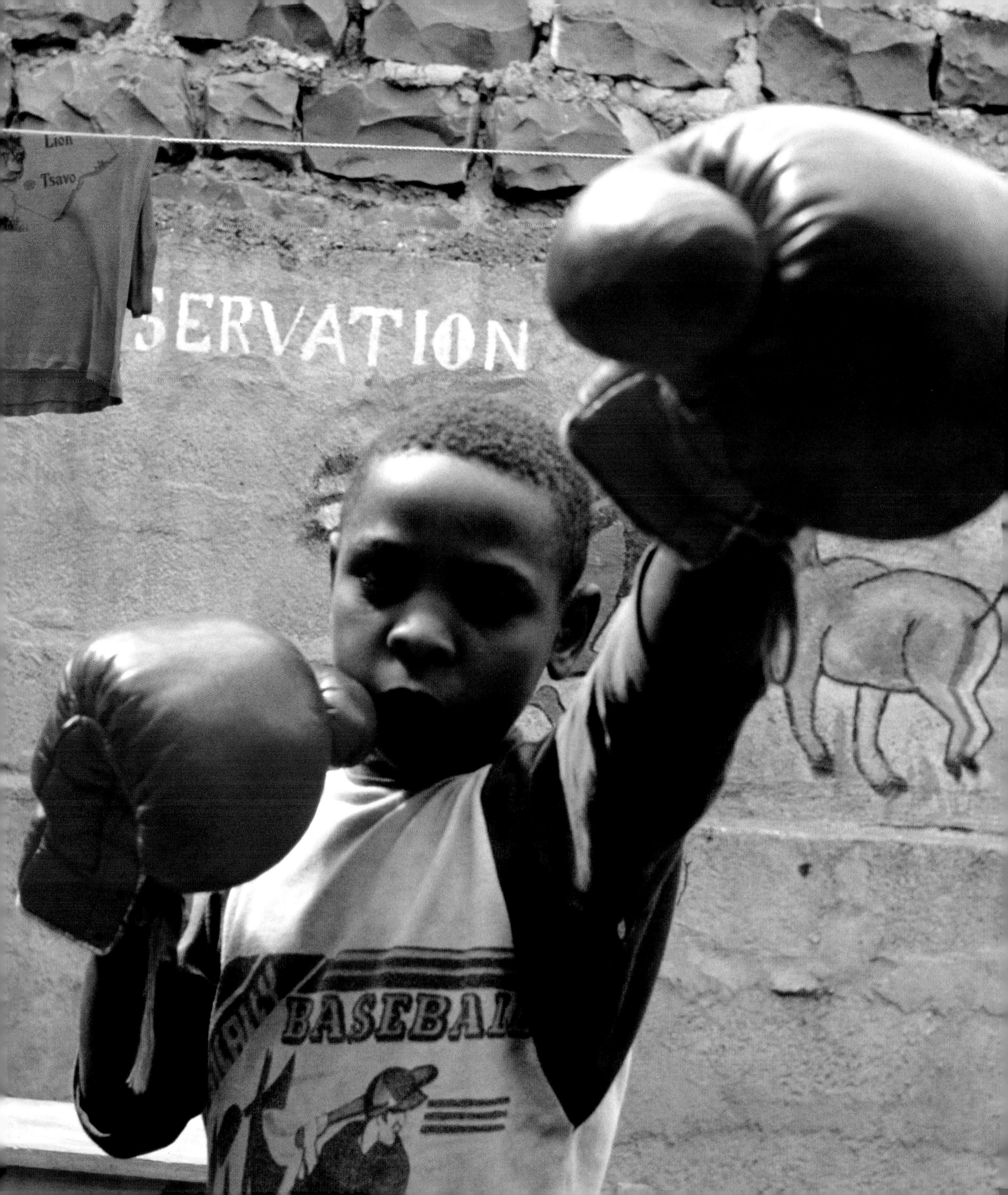
Lion
Tsavo
SERVATION
BASEBAL

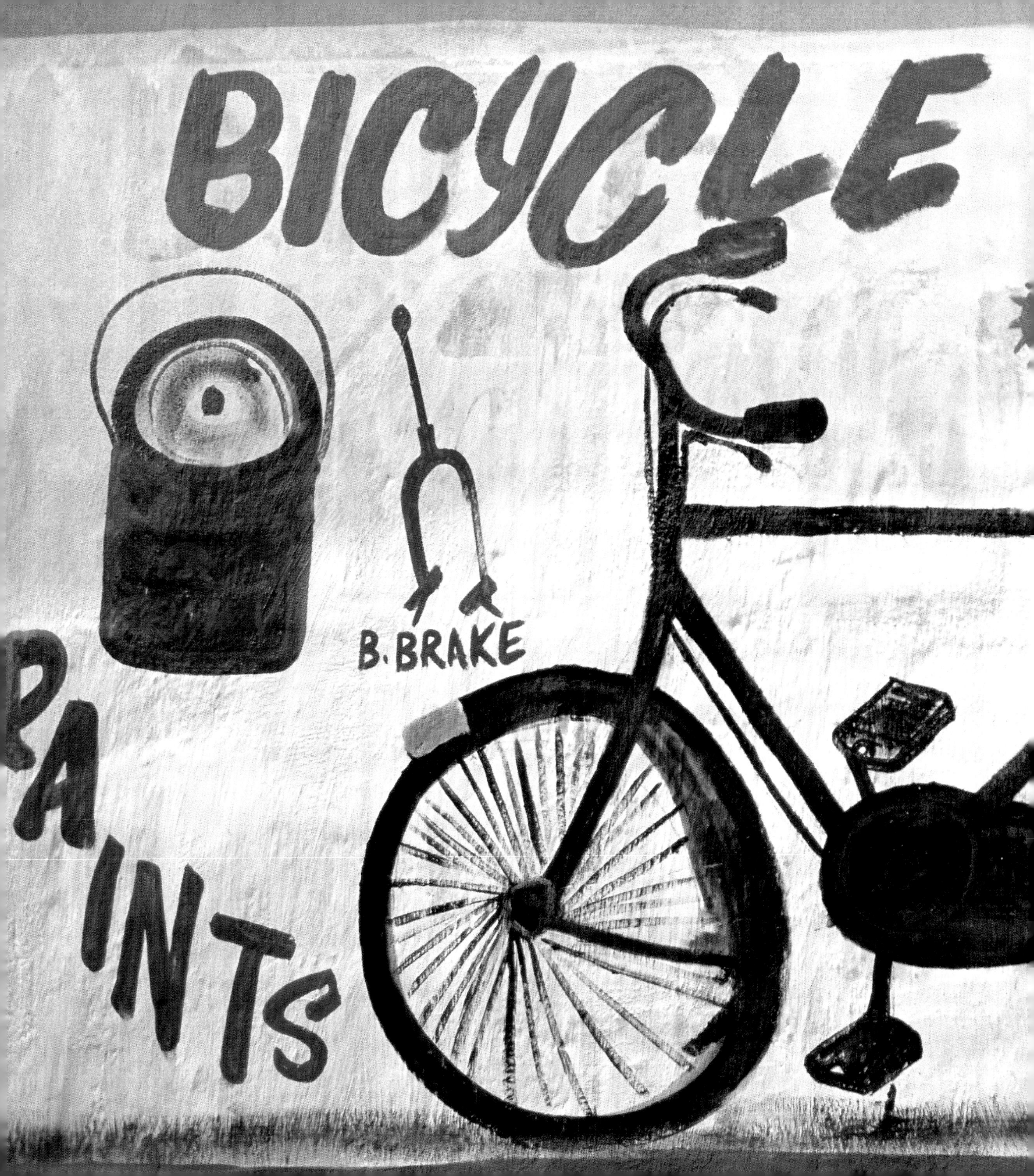
BICYCLE
B. BRAKE
PAINTS

SPARES

FREE-WHEEL, THINNER

JEMBE

DRAWER PULLERS

Mombasa has all the look of a picture of Paradise, painted by a small child. The deep Sea-arm round the island forms an ideal harbour; the land is made out of whitish coral-cliff grown with broad green mango trees and fantastic bald grey Baobab trees. The Sea at Mombasa is a blue as a cornflower, and, outside the inlet to the harbour, the long breakers of the Indian Ocean draw a thin crooked white line, and give out a low thunder even in the calmest weather. The narrow-streeted town of Mombasa is all built from coral-rock, in pretty shades of buff, rose and ochre, and above the town rises the massive old Fortress, with walls and embrasure, where three hundred years ago the Portuguese and the Arabs held out against one another; it displays stronger colours than the town, as if it had, in the course of the ages, from its high site drunk in more than one stormy sunset.

The sun seemed still high and bright to me, but I was not yet familiar with the sudden sunsets on the equator. Soon the sky was tinged with red and purples, as if a vast fire had been lit just below the horizon. The rare clouds became rimmed with gold, while the sun, orange and round like an incandescent coin, moved lower and lower and was gone. I had time to see the uncanny indigo expanse of the Indian Ocean, flat as a mirror, rippled only around the coral barrier. Palm trees darkened fast, car lights appeared on the thin tarmac road, and it was night.

I Dreamed of Africa Kuki Gallmann